Blend Your Own Pipe Tobacco:

52 recipes with 52 color labels

by Robert C.A. Goff

Dreamsplice
Christiansburg, Virginia

Dreamsplice
3462 Dairy Road
Christiansburg, VA 24073

www.dreamsplice.com

ISBN: 978-0-9761559-6-6

Contents

Acknowledgments

As I write this, I am 70 years old. So the list of those individuals who have contributed to my enjoyment and understanding of pure tobacco pipe blends over the past half-century could easily fill these brief pages. I will leave out most, and expect that they will never notice the slight. I will, however, offer a salute to my late friend, Lance Meagher, who first introduced me to English and Balkan style pipe tobaccos so long ago. Also to those no longer on this earth, I owe a debt to Craig Tarler, of Cornell & Diehl, whose sage advice guided my earliest blending efforts.

Over the years, I have personally grown over 100 distinct varieties of tobacco—a scant sampling of the thousands that exist. Some of the more rare varieties were grown from seed graciously provided by Paul Wicklund, of NorthwoodSeeds.com. In addition, Don Carey, of WholeLeafTobacco.com has generously offered me many dozens of samples of unique, commercial tobaccos, straight from the bale or barrel, to evaluate and enjoy. And Anton Eise de Vries, of CdF Domitab, has shared personal samples and seed, first from Indonesia, and subsequently from the Dominican Republic. Likewise, members of the FairTradeTobacco.com forum have happily shared many other varieties of seed, finished leaf that they either grew themselves, or that came into their hands from other forum members from across the world, and even samples of their own personal blends. These latter folks are too numerous to list, so I hope they will forgive my omission.

With the assistance of a number of other brave souls, I developed over the last decade, techniques for home tobacco kilning and kiln construction, home tobacco flue-curing (initially using a steel trash can!), home fire-curing, making small-batch Perique and making Cavendish on a kitchen stove. My attempt at making Latakia at home was a failure, since Latakia's distinctive aroma depends on smoke from woods that are not available to me. While I feel that I accomplished a lot with that list, much of my insight derived from the efforts—both successful and unsuccessful—of others.

Pure tobacco pipe blends are a constantly evolving exploration. Even the famed Balkan Sobranie Smoking Mixture—White (approximated by my *Balkan White* blend), evolved over the years of its success and availability, including changes in its proportion of Latakia. The collection of 52 pure tobacco pipe blends that I offer here is a snapshot of a single point in time. Tobaccos change, specific harvests differ, and smokers' tastes drift over the years. While these blends are my own, they are the fruit of input from numerous people over many years, and are informed by my past delight over fabulous commercial pipe blends that are no longer available in their original formulation.

R.C.A.G.

from the ruins of Tiahuanaco, Bolivia

Tobaccos

Any variety of tobacco can be used for pipe blending. Commercial pipe blends typically use only a handful of tobacco types, and process them using a variety of methods, and frequently add flavorants. While all commercial pipe tobacco blends use some manner of casing (typically glycerin or polypropylene glycol, or both), as a home blender, you can avoid casings altogether.

Types of tobacco were established by the USDA in the mid-to-late nineteenth century, based on marketing conditions at the time. So we have these classes:

- **Flue-cured** (nicknamed "Virginia"): relatively high sugar; moderate nicotine
- **Burley**: low sugar content; higher nicotine; higher pH (more alkaline); distinctive aroma
- **Maryland**: seedleaf derived; low sugar; somewhat higher pH; higher nicotine
- **Cigar Wrapper**: low sugar; higher pH; distinctive "cigar" aroma; can make suitable wrappers due to thinness, size and vein pattern
- **Cigar Binder**: low sugar; higher pH; distinctive "cigar" aroma; can make suitable binders due to stretch, tensile strength, size and vein pattern
- **Cigar Filler**: low sugar; higher pH; distinctive "cigar" aroma; not as suitable for wrapper or binder
- **Dark Air-cured**: high nicotine; large, thick leaf
- **Dark Fire-cured**: high nicotine; large, thick leaf; cured over smoldering oak
- **Oriental**: low nicotine; somewhat floral; smallish leaf; from the regions of the old Ottoman Empire (e.g. Balkans, Turkey, Greece, Middle-East)
- **Hungarian**: a collection of vastly differing types of tobacco from the regions of the old Austro-Hungarian Empire
- **Primitive**: huge category of tobacco that has undergone minimal agronomic development

Each of these classes may include scores or hundreds of distinct, named tobacco varieties. Belonging to a class depends on a set of vague characteristics common to that category.

In addition, pipe tobaccos are also categorized by their curing methods and further processing methods:

- **Air-cured**: typically cured in a ventilated barn. Most tobaccos that are not flue-cured or fire cured are air-cured prior to any further processing. Air-curing is sometimes referred to as "color-curing"--changing from fresh, green leaf to brown.
- **Flue-cured**: rapidly heat-cured over a 5 day period, ending at high temperatures (typically 165°F), resulting in "bright" leaf that is sweet, and ranges from light yellow to reddish brown. Only certain tobacco varieties can be successfully flue-cured. Because tobacco that has been flue-cured tends to be acidic, the nicotine in its smoke is not easily available for absorption by the membranes of the mouth and nasopharynx. Smoke from pure flue-cured leaf must be drawn into the lungs in order to allow absorption of its nicotine.
- **Fire-cured**: Any tobacco can be fire-cured. American-style fire-cured tobaccos typically use Dark Fire-cured tobacco, and are exposed to intense smoke from smoldering oak planks and sawdust. **Latakia** is a group of fire-cured Oriental varieties (often a yellow Basma type), exposed to months of smoke from selected Mediterranean woods, including Mediterranean pine sprigs as well as *Pistachia lentiscus*, the source of mastic ("tears of Chios"), which give the final, nearly black product a distinctive, "soapy", incense aroma. Latakia is now produced almost exclusively in Cyprus.
- **Perique**: Any variety of tobacco that is pressed under at least 30 psi and maintained beneath a liquid seal (creating anaerobic conditions) will gradual, over a period of at least 3 months, be modified by the yeast, *Pichia anomala*. This creates a higher pH (alkaline), and a fruity, earthy

and sometimes barnyard aroma. Its high pH is used to eliminate the tongue bite of the more acidic flue-cured leaf. The higher pH also increases nicotine absorption from the mouth and nasopharynx. Selection of tobacco variety will determine the actual nicotine content of resulting Perique.

- **Cavendish**: Any variety of tobacco that is cooked in the presence of boiling water or steam is converted into a Cavendish tobacco. Prolonged cooking and increased wetness leads to darker or nearly black Cavendish. (The term, "Cavendish", is also used to describe a type of shred, namely slices of a pressed plug. Cavendish-cut tobacco may or may not be cut from Cavendish processed tobacco.)
- **Pressed Plug**: Any variety of tobacco, or combination of varieties derived from any processing method can be layered as whole or partial leaf, then pressed into a flat "cake", often about 1 inch thick. Plug is typically cut into blocks of any length, and a width of 1 to 1-1/2 inches. When such a block is then thinly sliced, the product is called flake. Flake that is then separated into its individual shreds is called "rubbed" or "ready-rubbed".
- **Press Cake**: This is a firm (plank-like) plug of a tobacco blend made by pressing a previously blended shred. It is used by breaking off a small chunk, then crumbling it into a pipe bowl.
- **Twist**: Instead of pressing leaf, it can be twisted into a long rope of tobacco to the same effect. Sliced twist yields "coins" of the tobacco of the blend.
- **Kilned**: Heating tobacco in a container that maintains its humidity may greatly accelerate changes that occur during natural aging. Typical kiln conditions are ~125-128°F, relative humidity over 60%, continued for 4 to 6 weeks.

Pipe tobacco blends are crudely divided into "aromatic" and "non-aromatic". The former involves adding flavorants, and will not be discussed. Non-aromatic tobaccos are further grouped into:

- **English-style**: Earlier English law, in an effort to eliminate adulterants in commercial tobacco, forbade the use of any chemicals, flavorants or non-tobacco ingredients. This is a vaguely defined grouping.
- **Balkan**: An English-style tobacco blend that includes Latakia and an Oriental may be called a Balkan Blend.
- **Virginia-Perique** (VaPer): Made exclusively from Perique plus one of the many variations of flue-cured Virginia tobacco, VaPer blends adjust their apparent strength by the play of pH differences between the alkaline Perique and the acidic flue-cured.
- **American Burley Blends**: The presence of Burley is their only commonality. Any other tobacco types may be included.
- **Cavendish Blends**: While Cavendish may be included in any blend, those in which the chosen Cavendish dominates the blend might be considered a "Cavendish Blend".

Consumers can purchase whole leaf tobacco of various sorts (for example, from www.wholeleaftobacco.com). This includes, at present, Perique as well. Cavendish is generally considered a "tobacco product", and so is not sold by whole leaf retailers. I have included general instructions on making both Cavendish and Perique using the starting leaf you choose.

The Pipe Blends

Burley Latakia Matrix (in decreasing Latakia %)

Burley Bomb	75.00%
Mt. Burley	50.00%
Kentucky River	37.50%
Burley Baby	25.00%

Latakia Matrix (in decreasing Latakia %)

Davy Jones	75.00%
Siege of Acre	62.50%
Master's Mate	50.00%
Oud	43.75%
Saz	37.50%
Turkish Muse	37.50%
Towers of Antioch	37.50%
Balkan White	37.50%
Damascus Sun	31.25%
Smyrna Bright	25.00%

Perique Latakia Matrix (in decreasing Latakia %)

Boggy Night	50.00%
Angry Alligator	43.75%
Smiling Toad	37.50%
Cajun Muse	37.50%
Cypress Knee	37.50%
Spanish Moss	31.25%
Pearl of Shibam	25.00%

Ottoman Series (in decreasing Latakia %)

Janissary	75.00%
Sublime Port	50.00%
Mamluk	33.33%
Grand Vizier	25.00%
Vizier	0.00%

Open Series (in decreasing Latakia %)

Warspur	35.00%
Rich Creek	30.00%
Rosy Cheeks	29.00%
Chaptico	25.00%
Jewel of Macedonia	25.00%
Christmas 2018	18.75%
Flight Surgeon Deluxe	12.50%
Burley Virginia Blend Base	0.00%
Delilah	0.00%
Harpers Ferry	0.00%
Lancaster	0.00%
Semibreve	0.00%
Tercios	0.00%
Twice as Bright	0.00%

The blends presented here are loosely grouped into several series, as shown in the table to the left. Since most of the blends, though not all, contain some portion of Latakia, each of the first four series presents a generally similar aroma, unique to its series, but varying most noticeably by the percentage of Latakia contained. Some pipe smokers always prefer a specific range of Latakia in their blends, while others tend to begin the day with lighter Latakia, gradually progressing to a blend containing their preferred maximum Latakia as the last pipe in the evening.

A point of confusion may arise from the terminology used in various flue-cured Virginia ingredients. It is helpful to understand that all tobacco plants produce milder, lighter-colored, thinner, less flavorful, but more combustible leaf toward the bottom of the stalk, and progressively stronger, darker, thicker, more flavorful, less combustible leaf toward the top of the stalk. (With cigars, we have, from mildest to strongest, *volado, seco, viso, ligero*.) As this relates to flue-cured tobaccos, the very lowest leaf, called first priming, burns especially well, but is relatively flavorless. Moving up the stalk-- and generalizing, we have "Lemon Virginia", "Virginia Bright" and then "Virginia Red". The term, "Bright" also refers to any Virginia variety that has been flue-cured. Virginia Red can vary from reddish yellow to deep orange. Virginia Bright that has been subjected to additional flue-curing may be referred to as "Double-Bright".

Likewise, there are dozens of Oriental varieties. Although most are relatively mild, some are lighter-colored and milder, while others may be much darker and stronger. Only experimentation will inform you about your preferences here.

The table on the following pages is first sorted by blend series (labeled as Blend Group), and then alphabetically by blend name. The given "parts per 16 parts" are often approximate.

Name	Blend Group	Ingredients
Burley Baby	Burley	Latakia 25% (4 of 16 parts) Oriental 12.5% (2 of 16 parts) Virginia Bright 18.75% (3 of 16 parts) Virginia Red 18.75% (3 of 16 parts) Dark Air 6.25% (1 of 16 parts) Burley 18.75% (3 of 16 parts)
Burley Bomb	Burley	Latakia 75% (12 of 16 parts) Oriental 6.25% (1 of 16 parts) Burley 18.75% (3 of 16 parts)
Kentucky River	Burley	Latakia 37.5% (6 of 16 parts) Oriental 6.25% (1 of 16 parts) Virginia Bright 12.5% (2 of 16 parts) Virginia Red 18.75% (3 of 16 parts) Dark Air 6.25% (1 of 16 parts) Burley 18.75% (3 of 16 parts)
Mt. Burley	Burley	Latakia 50% (8 of 16 parts) Oriental 6.25% (1 of 16 parts) Virginia Bright 6.25% (1 of 16 parts) Virginia Red 6.25% (1 of 16 parts) Dark Air 6.25% (1 of 16 parts) Burley 25% (4 of 16 parts)
Black Mammoth Cavendish Blend	Cavendish	Burley Virginia Blend Base 90% (~14.5 of 16 parts) Black Mammoth Cavendish 10% (~1.5 of 16 parts)
Burley and Bright Cavendish Blend	Cavendish	Burley Red Tip Cavendish 33.33% (~5.25 of 16 parts) Virginia Bright Cavendish 66.67% (10.75 of 16 parts)
Burley Red Tips Cavendish Blend	Cavendish	Burley Virginia Blend Base 66.67% (~10.5 of 16 parts) Burley Red Tip Cavendish 33.33% (5.5 of 16 parts)
Harrow Velvet Cavendish Blend	Cavendish	Burley Virginia Blend Base 50% (8 of 16 parts) Harrow Velvet Cavendish [burley Cavendish] 50% (8 of 16 parts)
Maryland Cavendish Blend	Cavendish	Burley Virginia Blend Base 75% (12 of 16 parts) Maryland Cavendish 25% (4 of 16 parts)
Silver River Cavendish Blend	Cavendish	Burley Virginia Blend Base 85% (~13.5 of 16 parts) Silver River Cavendish 15% (~2.5 of 16 parts)
Virginia Bright Cavendish Blend	Cavendish	Burley Virginia Blend Base 75% (12 of 16 parts) Virginia Bright Cavendish 25% (4 of 16 parts)
Virginia Bright with Perique	Cavendish	Virginia Bright Cavendish 87.5% (14 of 16 parts) Perique 12.5% (2 of 16 parts)
Balkan White	Latakia	Latakia 37.5% (6 of 16 parts) Xanthi or Yenidje 12.5% (2 of 16 parts) Lemon Virginia 25% (4 of 16 parts) Virginia Red 18.75% (3 of 16 parts) Dark Air 6.25% (1 of 16 parts)
Damascus Sun	Latakia	Latakia 31.25% (5 of 16 parts) Oriental 18.75% (3 of 16 parts) Lemon Virginia 12.5% (2 of 16 parts) Virginia Red 31.25% (5 of 16 parts) Dark Air 6.25% (1 of 16 parts)

Name	Type	Blend
Davy Jones	Latakia	Latakia 75% (12 of 16 parts) Oriental 6.25% (1 of 16 parts) Lemon Virginia 6.25% (1 of 16 parts) Virginia Red 12.5% (2 of 16 parts)
Master's Mate	Latakia	Latakia 50% (8 of 16 parts) Oriental 12.5% (2 of 16 parts) Lemon Virginia 6.25% (1 of 16 parts) Virginia Red 25% (4 of 16 parts) Dark Air 6.25% (1 of 16 parts)
Oud	Latakia	Latakia 43.75% (7 of 16 parts) Oriental 12.5% (2 of 16 parts) Lemon Virginia 12.5% (2 of 16 parts) Virginia Red 25% (4 of 16 parts) Dark Air 6.25% (1 of 16 parts)
Saz	Latakia	Latakia 37.5% (6 of 16 parts) Oriental 12.5% (2 of 16 parts) Virginia Red 43.25% (7 of 16 parts) Dark Air 6.25% (1 of 16 parts)
Siege of Acre	Latakia	Latakia 62.5% (10 of 16 parts) Oriental 12.5% (2 of 16 parts) Virginia Red 18.75% (3 of 16 parts) Dark Air 6.25% (1 of 16 parts)
Smyrna Bright	Latakia	Latakia 25% (4 of 16 parts) Oriental 12.5% (2 of 16 parts) Lemon Virginia 31.25% (5 of 16 parts) Virginia Red 25% (4 of 16 parts) Dark Air 6.25% (1 of 16 parts)
Towers of Antioch	Latakia	Latakia 37.5% (6 of 16 parts) Oriental 12.5% (2 of 16 parts) Lemon Virginia 25% (4 of 16 parts) Virginia Red 18.75% (3 of 16 parts) Dark Air 6.25% (1 of 16 parts)
Atacama	open	mild Havana lug 33% (5.3 of 16 parts) Oriental 33% (~5.3 of 16 parts) Latakia 33 % (~5.3 of 16 parts)
Balkan Baldio	open	Mild Burley 50% (8 of 16 parts) Oriental 25% (4 of 16 parts) Latakia 25% (4 of 16 parts)
Basma Pastry Party	open	Basma 40% (~6.4 of 16 parts) Virginia Bright 25% (4 of 16 parts) Virginia Red 15% (~2.4 of 16 parts) Perique 20% (3.2 of 16 parts)
************************** Burley Virginia Blend Base** **************************	open	Burley Red Tips 33.3% (~5.3 of 16 parts) Virginia Bright 33.3% (~5.3 of 16 parts) Virginia Red 33.3% (~5.3 of 16 parts)
Chaptico '72	open	Virginia Red 50% (8 of 16 parts) Latakia 25% (4 of 16 parts) Kilned Maryland 25% (4 of 16 parts)
Christmas 2018	open	Virginia Double-Bright 37.5% (6 of 16 parts) Prilep [light Oriental] 25% (4 of 16 parts) Perique 12.5% (2 of 16 parts) Latakia 18.75% (3 of 16 parts) Pennsylvania (cigar leaf) 6.25% (1 of 16 parts)

Delilah	open	Samsun 62.5% (10 of 16 parts) Perique 25% (4 of 16 parts) Virginia Bright 12.5% (2 of 16 parts)
Flight Surgeon Deluxe	open	Perique 12.5% (2 of 16 parts) Düzce (mild Oriental) 25% (4 of 16 parts) Latakia 12.5% (2 of 16 parts) Kilned Maryland 12.5% (2 of 16 parts) Virginia Red 18.75% (3 of 16 parts) Virginia Bright Cavendish 18.75% (3 of 16 parts)
Harpers Ferry	open	Kilned Maryland 66.7% (~10.6 of 16 parts) Virginia Bright 33.3% (~5.3 of 16 parts)
Jewel of Macedonia	open	Latakia 25% (4 of 16 parts) Virginia Bright 40% (6.4 of 16 parts) Oriental 20% (3.2 of 16 parts) Perique 10% (1.6 of 16 parts) Black Cavendish 5% (0.8 of 16 parts)
Lancaster	open	Burley Virginia Blend Base 50% (8 of 16 parts) Dark Pennsylvania seedleaf [cigar leaf] 50% (8 of 16 parts)
Rich Creek	open	Light Burley 20% (3.2 of 16 parts) Dark Burley 20% (3.2 of 16 parts) Latakia 30% (4.8 of 16 parts) Oriental 30% (4.8 of 16 parts)
Rosy Cheeks	open	Latakia 29% (~4.6 of 16 parts) Virginia Red 26% (~4.2 of 16 parts) Oriental 18% (~2.9 of 16 parts) Virginia Bright 15% (2.4 of 16 parts) Dark Air 6% (~1 of 16 parts) Perique 6% (~1 of 16 parts)
Semibreve	open	Burley Cavendish 50% (8 of 16 parts) Virginia Bright 50% (8 of 16 parts)
Tercios	open	Virginia Bright 33.3% (~5.3 of 16 parts) Cavendish 33.3% (~5.3 of 16 parts) Perique 33.3% (~5.3 of 16 parts)
Twice as Bright	open	Virginia Double-Bright 66.7% (~10.7 of 16 parts) Perique 33.3% (~5.3 of 16 parts)
Warspur	open	Air-cured Virginia 30% (4.8 of 16 parts) Latakia 35% (5.6 of 16 parts) Oriental 30% (4.8 of 16 parts) Dark Air 5% (~0.8 of 16 parts)
Grand Vizier	Ottoman	Burley Virginia Blend Base 50% (8 of 16 parts) Light Oriental 25% (4 of 16 parts) Latakia 25% (4 of 16 parts)
Janissary	Ottoman	Burley Virginia Blend Base 25% (4 of 16 parts) Latakia 75% (12 of 16 parts)
Mamluk	Ottoman	Burley Virginia Blend Base 33.3% (~5.3 of 16 parts) Oriental 33.3% (~5.3 of 16 parts) Latakia 33.3% (~5.3 of 16 parts)
Sublime Port	Ottoman	Burley Virginia Blend Base 25% (4 of 16 parts) Oriental 25% (4 of 16 parts) Latakia 50% (8 of 16 parts)

Turkish Muse	Ottoman	Latakia 37.5% (6 of 16 parts) Oriental 12.5% (2 of 16 parts) Virginia Bright 12.5% (2 of 16 parts) Virginia Red 31.25% (5 of 16 parts) Dark Air 6.25% (1 of 16 parts)
Vizier	Ottoman	Burley Virginia Blend Base 75% (12 of 16 parts) Light Oriental 25% (4 of 16 parts)
Angry Alligator	Perique	Latakia 43.75% (7 of 16 parts) Oriental 12.5% (2 of 16 parts) Virginia Bright 12.5% (2 of 16 parts) Virginia Red 18.75% (3 of 16 parts) Perique 12.5% (2 of 16 parts)
Boggy Night	Perique	Latakia 50% (8 of 16 parts) Oriental 12.5% (2 of 16 parts) Virginia Bright 6.25% (1 of 16 parts) Virginia Red 25% (4 of 16 parts) Perique 6.25% (1 of 16 parts)
Cajun Muse	Perique	Latakia 37.5% (6 of 16 parts) Oriental 12.5% (2 of 16 parts) Virginia Bright 12.5% (2 of 16 parts) Virginia Red 25% (4 of 16 parts) Perique 12.5% (2 of 16 parts)
Cypress Knee	Perique	Latakia 37.5% (6 of 16 parts) Oriental 12.5% (2 of 16 parts) Virginia Bright 25% (4 of 16 parts) Virginia Red 18.75% (3 of 16 parts) Perique 6.25% (1 of 16 parts)
Pearl of Shibam	Perique	Latakia 25% (4 of 16 parts) Oriental 25% (4 of 16 parts) Lemon Virginia 31.25% (5 of 16 parts) Perique 18.75% (3 of 16 parts)
Samsun Bright	Perique	Latakia 25% (4 of 16 parts) Samsun 8% (~1.25 of 16 parts) Virginia Bright 36% (~6 of 16 parts) Virginia Red 23% (~3.5 of 16 parts) Perique 8% (~1.25 of 16 parts)
Smiling Toad	Perique	Latakia 37.5% (6 of 16 parts) Oriental 18.75% (3 of 16 parts) Virginia Red 25% (4 of 16 parts) Perique 18.75% (3 of 16 parts)
Spanish Moss	Perique	Latakia 31.25% (5 of 16 parts) Oriental 18.75% (3 of 16 parts) Virginia Bright 18.75% (3 of 16 parts) Virginia Red 12.5% (2 of 16 parts) Perique 12.5% (2 of 16 parts) Dark Air 6.25% (1 of 16 parts)

The blend labels at the end of this book may be cut out and attached to the containers of your choice. You may alternatively copy the label images for use. (See the Creative Commons license information on the copyright page.)

All of the blend labels are displayed alphabetically by blend name.

the closer an arm notch is to the wall, the greater the applied weight

Piston

Multiply the dimensions of the top surface of the pressed tobacco, to get surface area in square inches. **Pressure** = the weight exerted at the "piston" divided by the surface area.

If the top surface of the folded Ziplock bag is 3" x 6", then its surface area is:
    18 in^2.
If we apply 65 pounds at the "piston", then the **pressure = 65/18 = 3.6 psi.**

1 gallon water jug

Pressing a shredded pipe blend within a 1-quart Ziplock bag, using a wall-mounted press. Pressing between two planks weighted with several heavy objects also works, but takes longer to consolidate the press cake. The lever arm press allows the 8 pound jug to exert 65 pounds at the "piston".

Making Cavendish

Cavendish is essentially stewed or steamed tobacco. The process darkens the leaf color and also dramatically alters the flavor, burn characteristics and aroma. The Cavendish process has practically no effect on nicotine levels.

The most basic method is to place color-cured leaf into a large colander that is nested inside a large pot, suspending the tobacco above boiling water. Such an approach requires 8 or more hours to sufficiently darken leaf.

A faster method is to bundle and pack very damp leaf into Mason jars, one jar for each variety, and pressure-cook the sealed jars, typically for about 5 hours. Once cooled, the tobacco can either be removed and dried for use, or simply left in the jar indefinitely, since it has been sterilized, and cannot mold.

The temperature of cooking (212°F for steaming or with a hot water bath, versus 249°F when pressure-cooked at 15 psi) and the duration seem to have less influence on the final color than how wet the leaf is during cooking: the wetter the darker.

Cavendish tobacco dries out slowly. So be sure to allow it sufficient time to dry-down, before storing it.

The Cavendish process is remarkably successful at taming the varieties that you choose. With Bright leaf, the pH is slightly increased, so in blends with Perique, you should require less of the latter to eliminate tongue bite.

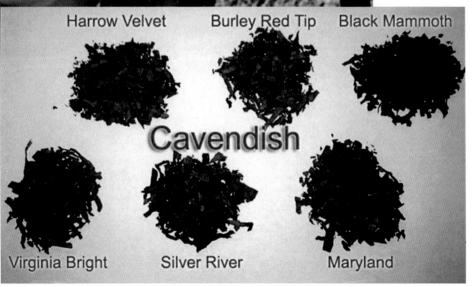

Harrow Velvet   Burley Red Tip   Black Mammoth

Cavendish

Virginia Bright   Silver River   Maryland

Tongue Bite

Pipe tobacco blends, as well as some pure varieties of tobacco can cause two distinct and meaningful (for blending) sensations. The most common meaning of "tongue bite" is a burning sensation near the tip of the tongue. There are two general causes of tip-of-the-tongue tongue bite.

The first is from smoking cased, commercial tobacco. The glycerin and polypropylene glycol added, in various concentrations, to all commercial pipe tobaccos now, cause a chemical tongue bite. In the same manner, most tobacco flavorants (e.g. hazelnut, cherry, vanilla, etc.) are manufactured and sold in water-soluble solutions of polypropylene glycol. While similar flavorants may be available as an oil, which may or may not cause tongue bite, their use requires that they be first dissolved in alcohol.

The second cause of *tongue-bite near the tip of the tongue is from tobacco smoke with a relatively higher acidity (lower pH)*. Pure flue-cured Virginia Bright is notorious for this. Most published remedies for this Virginia tongue bite is to "sip the smoke slowly". What that accomplishes is adequate time between small puffs for saliva to bathe the tongue, and neutralize the acidity. If your preference is for the "edgy" Virginia tongue bite from your pipe, then that is the only approach to mitigation.

A key to understanding the effect of particular Virginia tobaccos on tongue bite is to realize that the *higher the sugar content, the greater the potential tongue bite*. And this is directly related to the stalk level from which the Virginia is harvested. With the exception of the very bottom leaf ("first priming"), which has little sweetness, the lower leaf is sweeter than the upper leaf. So on a progression from sweetest (greatest tongue bite) to least sweet (least tongue bite), flue-cured Virginia can be ranked as follows:

SWEETEST **[Lemon | Bright | Double-bright | Virginia Red | Virginia Red Tips]** LEAST SWEET

The impact of this is that Lemon Virginia offers more tongue bite than Virginia Red. And blending of Lemon and Red tends to average the respective tongue bite of each component.

If, instead, you would like to use blending to eliminate tongue bite altogether, there is good news. That is where tongue bite that occurs at the sides and rear of the tongue (I'll call it "back-of-tongue bite") enters the picture. While lower pH (acidic) burns the tip of the tongue, higher pH (alkaline) causes back-of-tongue bite. Both are caused by pH imbalance, and those causes are the opposite of one another. If you can drive the acidity more toward a neutral pH, there simply is no tongue bite.

Relatively *alkaline tobaccos, such as Burley, Maryland, dark air cured and Perique – especially Perique, cause back-of-tongue bite.* These are tobaccos that typically have little sugar in the leaf lamina at harvest.

When you smoke a bowl of any tobacco blend, paying attention to the location on your tongue of tongue bite that you may experience will inform you as to how to improve the blend by eliminating that particular tongue bite. The simplest example is a straightforward Virginia and Perique (VaPer) blend. It's possible to achieve no bite with any Virginia mixed with any Perique. But as previously mentioned, each category of flue-cured Virginia has its own level of sweetness—that is, its own likelihood of causing tip-tongue bite. Similarly, differing batches of Perique sometimes vary in their alkalinity – differ in their likelihood of causing back-of-tongue bite. So, with our VaPer example, if it burns the tip of your tongue, add more Perique; if it burns the sides and back of your tongue, reduce the Perique.

My starting point for most of my Perique and Latakia blends is:

5 parts Lemon Virginia : 3 parts Perique

adjusting for types of Virginias and the Perique batch. *"Twice as Bright"* uses about 7:3.

Making Perique

Purchasing whole leaf Perique for your blending is considerably easier than making it, but every home tobacco grower should make at least one batch—just for the sense of self-confidence and self-reliance it instills. You can also make Perique from purchased burley, Maryland, Pennsylvania seedleaf, and other varieties.

Despite what you may read about St. James Parish Perique, anyone can make a delicious Perique from any tobacco variety. The nicotine strength of the final Perique will be determined by the nicotine content of the variety you choose.

Perique is tobacco that has been anaerobically (without oxygen) fermented by the yeast, *Pichia anomala*. It is sometimes referred to as "pressure-cured". This is true. The method uses a liquid-holding container and a press of some sort. Tobacco is placed into the container, a follower is added on top of that, and pressure is applied, until the cells of the leaf lamina are ruptured, and the leaf's liquid is expressed.

In the photos, I use an acrylic jar and a polypropylene follower (from a cheese mold). The press is a simple, hand-twisted clamp from a big box home improvement store. The leaf has been color-cured and stemmed or frog-legged.

The stories of requiring 6000 plus pounds of pressure are misreported. The traditional Perique pressing in large oak barrels does require about that much *weight*, but dividing that by the surface area of the follower reveals a far more modest *pressure* of 30 to 50 psi. The exact psi is not important. Also, in my tall jar, the amount of tobacco is unimportant, since the generated pressure is entirely a matter between the clamp force and the surface area of my plastic follower.

I mist the leaf, so that it is fully flexible, maybe slightly damp, pack it in, then apply the clamp.

Perique juice after 2 days

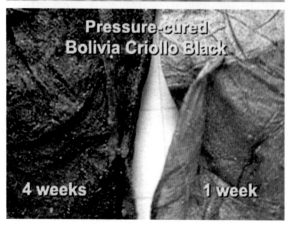

Pressure-cured
Bolivia Criollo Black

4 weeks   1 week

The chunk of wood (a segment from a fence post) allows me to use the clamp on this tall jar with a small amount of tobacco. The clamp is tightened until a scant amount of liquid (usually relatively colorless) seals the gap between the follower and the wall of the jar. This setup should be placed in a "room temperature" environment. Too much heat will favor a barnyard aroma, while too little heat will dramatically slow the fermentation.

The liquid seal must be maintained for the duration of Perique curing, and replenished with a bit of water if needed. After a couple of days, nicotine contained by the laminar juice oxidizes to a dark brown.

The entire process of pressing under a liquid seal must continue for at least 3 months. The final color of the leaf will be darker if you release the press after 1 or 2 weeks, completely remove all the tobacco, tease it apart and spread it to air for an hour or so, then replace it, replenishing the liquid seal, and reapplying pressure. This brief oxygen exposure further oxidizes nicotine, but does not confuse the microbial growth within the pressed mass. This "airing" can be repeated a time or three over the duration of the cure.

To begin with, all sorts of random microbes will grow within the pressed mass of wet tobacco. So the aromas will change as time passes. After a month or two, perhaps longer, the *Pichia anomala* yeast will begin to completely take over the fermentation process and the microbial population. At this point, a deep, "grapey", fruity aroma will dominate. A bit of "barnyard" is not unusual. If your batch has reached this aroma milestone by 3 months, then you can either continue further fermentation or end the process.

The new Perique should be spread and aired, and allowed to fully dry, prior to storage—to avoid mold, or it can be stored soggy wet in a thick plastic bag within the refrigerator.

Shredding, Blending and Storage

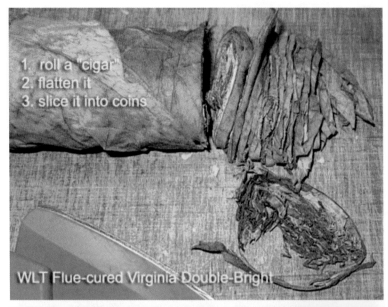

1. roll a "cigar"
2. flatten it
3. slice it into coins

WLT Flue-cured Virginia Double-Bright

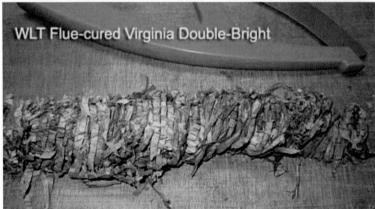

WLT Flue-cured Virginia Double-Bright

WLT Flue-cured Virginia Double-Bright

4. cut coins into 3 pieces

The width of pipe tobacco shred influences the burn rate and temperature. You can use any shred you choose, but blending is considerably more efficient if the components are all of roughly the same shred width and length. A fine shred will burn hotter and faster.

Leaf should be brought to a somewhat flexible condition – brought "into Case", and the stem removed. If you have a tobacco shredder (power or hand-cranked), then that is your easiest choice. If you don't have a shredder, or prefer a coarser shred than your shredded can provide, there are other relatively efficient approaches.

Hand shredding is simplified by compacting the leaf in some way – either as a pressed block, or as a rolled "cigar" of leaf. The latter is the quickest. I simply roll up the leaf of one variety, slice the roll, cut the resulting coins, then rub out the shred.

The shredded leaf of each blend component is measured into a 1 gallon Ziplock bag—which is then inflated, and agitated for about 60 seconds, until well blended. Most blends will alter their character subtly during the few hours after blending.

I use a **6" Kuhn Rikon Kulu Knife** for all my shredding (and as a chaveta for cigar making). I hold it not by its handle, but by the riser, near the blade, with the handle extending away from my hand. This allows me to exert considerable pressure.

WLT Flue-cured Virginia Double-Bright

5. rub out the shred

Twice as Bright

Double-bright 2/3
Perique 1/3

16 ounce polystyrene (food grade) jars

recycled tin

Your blended pipe tobacco should never be stored damp—that is, it should **not** "feel" like commercial pipe tobacco. It needs to be humid enough to not crumble when handled. Any greater moisture content will encourage the rapid growth of mold. Besides, you want it to be nearly dry when you smoke it. Tobacco that is too moist can often just be left in the blending bag, with the bag open for as long as required to dry-down.

Standard polyethylene sandwich bags are too permeable to water *vapor* to be used for tobacco storage for more than a day or two. The heavier, "freezer" Ziplocks provide a much better vapor barrier, useful for holding a small batch for a week or more.

Empty commercial tobacco tins are good for short-term storage of a small batch. The width of a 16 ounce polystyrene jar, which seals fairly well, makes it easy to fill a pipe, without spilling tobacco. The advantage of using jars is that they stack well.

When following the blending recipes, you can be precise (using a digital scale and the percentages) or more casual, using the "parts of 16 parts". In the latter, one part can be a tablespoon, a gram, a pound, or a shoe-full. Too much precision may be disappointed by variations in the tobacco itself.

Angry Alligator

Latakia 43.5% VA Red 18.75%
Oriental 12.5% Bright 12.5% Perique 12.5%

Atacama

Mild Havana Lug 33%
Oriental 33% Latakia 33%

Balkan Baldio

Mild Burley 50% Oriental 25%
Latakia 25%

Balkan White

Latakia 37.5%   Oriental 12.50%
Bright 25.00%   VA Red 18.75%
Dark Air 6.25%

blank

Basma 40%   VA Bright 25%
VA Red 15%   Perique 20%

Black Mammoth

Cavendish
Blend

Burley Virginia Blend Base 90%
Kilned Black Mammoth Cavendish 10%

Latakia 50.00%   Oriental 12.50%
Bright   6.25%   VA Red 25.00%
          Perique 6.25%

Burley & Bright

The
Cavendish

Virginia Bright Cavendish 2/3
Kilned Burley Red Tip Cavendish 1/3

blank

Burley Baby

Latakia 25.00%	Burley 18.75%
Oriental 12.50%	Bright 18.75%
VA Red 18.75%	Dark Air 6.25%

Burley Bomb

Latakia	75.00%
Burley	18.75%
Oriental	6.25%

Burley Red Tip
FAIR TRADE TOBACCO
Cavendish
Blend

Burley Virginia Blend Base 2/3
Kilned Burley Red Tip Cavendish 1/3

Burley Virginia Blend Base

Burley Red Tips (kilned) 1/3
Flue-cured Virginia Bright 1/3
Flue-cured Virginia Red 1/3

blank

Cajun Muse

Latakia 37.5%   Oriental 12.5%
Bright 12.5%   VA Red 25.0%
Perique 12.5%

Chaptico '72

FAIR TRADE TOBACCO

Flue-cured Virginia Red 50%
Latakia 25%
Kilned Maryland 25%

Sperry Christmas 2018

FAIR TRADE TOBACCO

Double Bright VA 37.50%
Prilip   25.00%
Latakia   18.75%
Perique   12.50%
Pennsylvania leaf 6.25%

Cypress Knee

Latakia 37.50% Oriental 12.50%
Bright 25.00% VA Red 18.75%
Perique 6.25%

blank

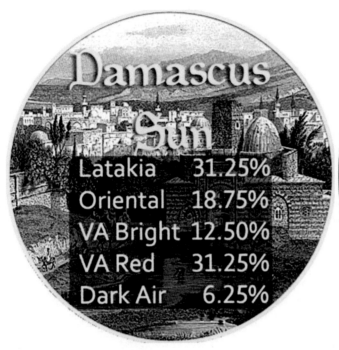

Damascus Sun

Latakia	31.25%
Oriental	18.75%
VA Bright	12.50%
VA Red	31.25%
Dark Air	6.25%

Davy Jones

Latakia	75%
Oriental	6.25%
Bright	6.25%
VA Red	12.50%

Delilah

Samsun 62.5%   Perique 25%   Bright 12.5%

Flight Surgeon Deluxe

Perique	12.50%
Düzce	25.00%
Latakia	12.50%
Maryland	12.50%
Virginia Red	18.75%
Virginia Cavendish	18.75%

blank

Grand Vizier

Burley Virginia Blend Base 50%
Light Oriental 25%
Latakia 25%

Ottoman Series

Harpers Ferry

Maryland 2/3 Bright 1/3

Harrow Velvet

FAIR TRADE
TOBACCO

Cavendish

Blend

Burley Virginia Blend Base 50%
Harrow Velvet Cavendish 50%

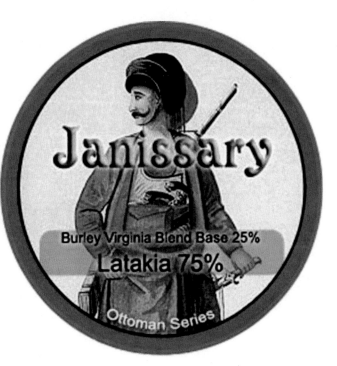

Janissary

Burley Virginia Blend Base 25%
Latakia 75%

Ottoman Series

blank

Latakia 25%   Bright 40%
Oriental 20%   Perique 10%
Black Cavendish 5%

Latakia 37.50%   Burley 18.75%
Oriental 6.25%   Bright 12.50%
VA Red 18.75%   Dark Air 6.25%

Burley Virginia Blend Base 50%
Dark Pennsylvania Seedleaf 50%

Burley Virginia Blend Base 1/3
Oriental 1/3   Latakia 1/3

blank

Maryland

FAIR TRADE T TOBACCO

Cavendish
Blend

Burley Virginia Blend Base 75%
Kilned Maryland Cavendish 25%

Master's Mate

Latakia 50%
Oriental 12.5%
Bright 6.25%
VA Red 25%
Dark Air 6.25%

Mt. Burley

Latakia 50.00%   Burley 25.00%
Oriental 6.25%   Bright 6.25%
VA Red 6.25%   Dark Air 6.25%

Latakia 43.75%; Oriental 12.50%; Bright 12.50%; VA Red 25%; Dark Air 6.25%

Oud

blank

PEARL OF SHIBAM

Lemon Virginia	31%
Oriental	25%
Cyprus Latakia	25%
Perique	19%

الشرق

Rich Creek

Light Burley 20%
Dark Burley 20%
Latakia 30%   Oriental 30%

Rosy Cheeks

Latakia 29%	VA Red 26%
Oriental 18%	Bright 15%
Dark Air 6%	Perique 6%

Samsun Bright

Virginia Bright 36% Virginia Red 23%
Latakia 25%
Samsun 8%   Perique 8%

blank

Saz

Latakia	37.50%
Oriental	12.50%
Virginia Red	43.75%
Dark Air	6.25%

Semibreve

4/4

Burley Cavendish 50%
Bright Virginia 50%

Siege of Acre (1799)

Latakia	62.50%
Oriental	12.50%
Va Red	18.75%
Dark Air	6.25%

Silver River Cavendish Blend

FAIR TRADE TOBACCO

Burley Virginia Blend Base 85%
Kilned Silver River Cavendish 15%

blank

Smiling Toad

Latakia	37.50%
VA Red	25.00%
Oriental	18.75%
Perique	18.75%

Smyrna Bright

Latakia	25.00%
Oriental	12.50%
VA Bright	31.25%
VA Red	25.00%
Dark Air	6.25%

Spanish Moss

Latakia, Virginia and Perique

Latakia 31.25%	Oriental 18.75%
Bright 18.75%	VA Red 12.50%
Perique 12.50%	Dark Air 6.25%

Sublime Port

Burley Virginia Blend Base 25%
Oriental 25%
Latakia 50%

Ottoman Series

blank

Tercios

Bright 1/3
Cavendish 1/3
Perique 1/3

Towers of Antioch

Latakia	37.50%
VA Bright	25.00%
VA Red	18.75%
Oriental	12.50%
Dark Air	6.25%

Turkish Muse

Latakia 37.5%; Oriental 12.5%; Bright 12.5%
VA Red 31.25%; Dark Air 6.25%

Twice as Bright

Double-Bright 2/3
Perique 1/3

blank

Virginia Bright

Cavendish

Blend

Burley Virginia Blend Base 75%
Virginia Bright Cavendish 25%

Virginia Cavendish

with

Perique

Flue-cured Virginia Bright Cavendish 87.5%
Perique 12.5%

Vizier

Smooth with medium-strength
Burley Virginia Blend Base 75%
Light Oriental 25%

Ottoman Series

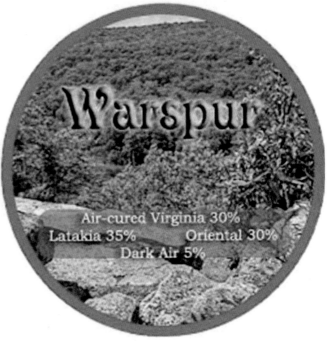

Warspur

Air-cured Virginia 30%
Latakia 35%   Oriental 30%
Dark Air 5%

blank

Bonus Blends

Edinburg	open	Oriental 50% (8 of 16 parts) Cavendish 30% (4.8 of 16 parts) Perique 10% (1.6 of 16 parts) Virginia Bright 10% (1.6 of 16 parts)
Super Blood Wolf Moon Eclipse	open	Virginia Red 25% (4 of 16 parts) Kilned Burley Red Tip 25% (4 of 16 parts) Virginia Red Cavendish 18.75% (3 of 16 parts) Burley Red Cavendish 18.75% (3 of 16 parts) Latakia 12.5% (2 of 16 parts)

Made in United States
Orlando, FL
23 November 2022

24895720R00027